To: Conrad & Warner

Embrace Freedom

Embrace Freedom

# A REAL LIFE FAIRY TALE
# PRINCESS DIANA

A REAL LIFE FAIRY TALE

# PRINCESS DIANA

Written by Emberli Pridham

Illustrated by Danilo Cerovic

Columbus, OH

A Real Life Fairy Tale Princess Diana

Published by Gatekeeper Press

2167 Stringtown Rd, Suite 109

Columbus, OH 43123-2989

www.GatekeeperPress.com

Library of Congress Control Number: 2022930962

ISBN (hardcover): 9781662911996

ISBN (paperback): 9781662912009

eISBN: 9781662912016

In the many years of my decorating career, I have had the distinct privilege of designing the interiors of resorts, hotels, castles, embassies, state houses, and residences all across the world and many with royal leanings. During the design stage, I have worked with many families with young daughters on the decorating of their bedrooms. The girls are usually aged between 5 and 8 and all are enamored with Lady Diana Spencer, the late Princess of Wales. I know that Diana is known the world over as the People's Princess and can never be replaced. In keeping with the respect and love for the Princess, Emberli Pridham has produced this charming book about Diana and her life to enchant children with her tale for years to come.

– Carleton Varney, President of Dorothy Draper & Company, Inc.

*This book is dedicated to my wonderful children who inspire me everyday.*

*– Emberli Pridham*

Once there was a girl named Diana Spencer,

a spunky little one who always played and had fun.

She had pretty eyes like bluebells and blonde hair like sunshine

that swayed in the wind when she liked to run.

She lived in Norfolk, England, with her father, mother, two sisters, and little brother.

They lived on land owned by the longest reigning Queen in history.

She was Queen Elizabeth II of the United Kingdom, a royal like no other.

The family home on the Queen's estate was called Park House.

Diana's family had been friends with the royals for many, many years.

Diana loved to play with the Queen's children.

They had many adventures, playing games and singing fun cheers.

One day, Diana's father became an Earl,

and thereafter Diana was called Lady Diana, even though she was still a young girl.

*L*ady Diana attended boarding school, where she excelled in ballet, music, and sports.

She liked to dance, sing, and enjoy life with her friends.

She still loved freedom just like when she was little, of course!

Then, she was off to finishing school
to learn proper manners;

however, Lady Diana chose another way!

She left school to live in London with friends
in an apartment called a flat.

And Lady Diana worked at a nursery school
and as a nanny to children each day.

One thing was true and would never change -

Lady Diana still loved to play with little
ones from any age.

Diana began a friendship with the Queen's son, Prince Charles of Wales.

He took Lady Diana to galas and charity dances.

Soon the Prince asked Lady Diana for her hand in marriage, and she gladly accepted.

Lady Diana moved to the royal Clarence House, where people gave her new and interesting glances.

The royal wedding was grand and glamourous,

with millions of spectators across the world.

Lady Diana's dress was long and white, her tiara shining with sparkling diamonds.

She became Princess Diana, a real life fairy tale for a once spunky young girl.

From the very beginning, she was adored and loved for her beauty and grace.

Her vow was to lead with compassion for everyone in every place.

$\mathcal{P}$rincess Diana began her royal work right away.

She traveled the globe to places like America, Africa, and India, to name a few.

She spread love and kindness to all those who crossed her path,

something that never left her feeling blue.

Children and adults loved her attention and kind heart.

Princess Diana gave everything she had to many good causes from the start.

$S$he was a member of 100 different charities,

   visiting the young from other countries and those who fell ill.

She was revered for her efforts and given praises,

   a princess known for her hard work and strong will.

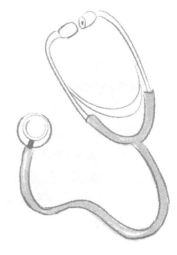

𝒫rincess Diana, who had loved children for so long,

was overjoyed when her own two little princes came along!

She named her boys Prince William and Prince Harry.

The oldest, William, had blonde hair and the youngest, Harry, had bright red.

She loved them whole-heartedly and dearly,

and kissed them each night before putting them to bed.

*P*rincess Diana was a wonderful and loving mother to her little princes.

She doted on them and brought them on travel and work trips.

She attended school events and always taught them to do their best,

watching them play in the garden as knights with toy swords in their grips.

They often visited Disney World and went skiing in the snow.

Her whole heart was centered on her two boys, as everyone would know.

*P*rincess Diana continued to meet people from all walks of life,

from the smallest of children to friends like actor John Travolta and musician Elton John, all while spreading empathy and hope for people to rely upon.

*P*rincess Diana's cherished story of love, patience, and grace is a legacy that will always live on.

Emberli Pridham grew up in Dallas, Texas inspired by her grandmother, an author, and a wonderful library of books. She, along with her husband David, are the co-authors of the Amazon best-selling STEM book series, *If Not You, Then Who?*, which aims to teach children about the inventions and patents in everyday life, inspiring and empowering them to imagine and create their own.

Emberli is currently writing the next two books about inspiring and influential people for the *Real Life Fairy Tale* series. She also spends her time taking care of her beautiful family and is extensively involved in philanthropic work on behalf of the Hasbro Children's Hospital, Dallas Museum of Art, Dallas Symphony, Elton John AIDS Foundation, and American Cancer Society, among other charities.

The Pridhams live in Dallas, Texas with their three ever-curious children Brooke, Noah, and Graham.

For more information visit reallifefairytale.com
Follow on Instagram @reallifefairytale

Photo Credit: Mariah Gale